*The greatest austerity is truthfulness
and the greatest journey is through your mind*

RETREAT INTO ETERNITY

an Upanishad—book of aphorisms

Swami Amar Jyoti

There is a story told from the mythology of India, and like all creation myths, it owes its origin to symbology not necessarily unrelated to reality. Brahmā, it is said, was all that existed long before the cosmos came into being. In a state of unmanifested Pure Consciousness He remained until the will arose within Him to manifest His blissfulness through creation. Out of Him the unmanifest took form and the universe with countless galaxies and universes within universes came into being. Brahmā was glad, yet still He wished to manifest Himself in a form that would contain all His supreme attributes, a likeness of Himself to live and play with Himself in creation. From that thought came the birth of man. Seven mortals were formed and placed on a world like our own to dwell there and remain fully conscious of their Source. But, as Brahmā had not anticipated, they immediately sat in meditation and merged back into their Creator. Having not

even a subtle thread of attachment to the manifested creation, their will to return back to their Source was supreme and they vanished. Brahmā then pondered this and decided to give man an added element, one which would keep the play continuing: individual desire. This desire gave the recreated mortals the possibility of individual consciousness, and when tempted with this singular freedom, Brahmā watched with delight and gradually gave them more and more line with which they wove themselves a fine veil of *māyā* (illusory perception). This veil gradually became thicker and thicker until finally they were caught in their own web, and left to enjoy their minds' desires and reap accordingly.

After some time, some of these mortals saw the folly of their individual freedom, and they sensed Brahmā's game. Dropping all identity to their separate selves, and through their supreme will with which, as sons of Brahmā they were endowed, they once again merged into the Pure Consciousness and All-Pervasiveness of their Source. But those who remained became further and further entrapped in the veil of illusion which, by separating themselves from their Creator, they had created. To their existence we owe the generations of this day.

●　●　●　●　●　●　●

The Vedic culture that has flourished in India for thousands of years brought to the civilization of man a nobility of purpose and knowledge of the three realms—physical, psychological and spiritual—not transcended to this day. All the mathematics and science attributed to later cultures owe their origin, directly or indirectly, to this flowering of humanity. All that science has so painstakingly learned, step by step, about the creation up to the present was known in a flash by these Vedic bards. How? By the simplest, most direct method—though not a method at all. The sages 'knew', by meditating on the Source of all things, that whatever exists in the cosmos, also exists as an identical microcosm within the human body. Understanding nature by its lowest denominator—what we call the atomic and subatomic levels, and was to them *ātman* — they 'knew' the All-Pervading Reality.

These *rishīs* (sages), as they were called, revealed their vast knowledge in the Upanishads, the end portion of the Vedas, comprising the Essential Knowledge as it was spoken to their disciples. Precise, enlightening aphorisms they uttered, and with the power inherent in these truths, mortals through the ages have been freed from the bondage of ignorance.

That which is most subtle may or may not show abrupt apparent change, but slowly, imperceptibly, like the unfathomable canyon carved by the river out of solid rock, like the first light of dawn gradually transforming to radiant sun, the words of the Illumined Ones change our lives, and lovingly, purposefully lift our souls back to the Source from which we came.

4

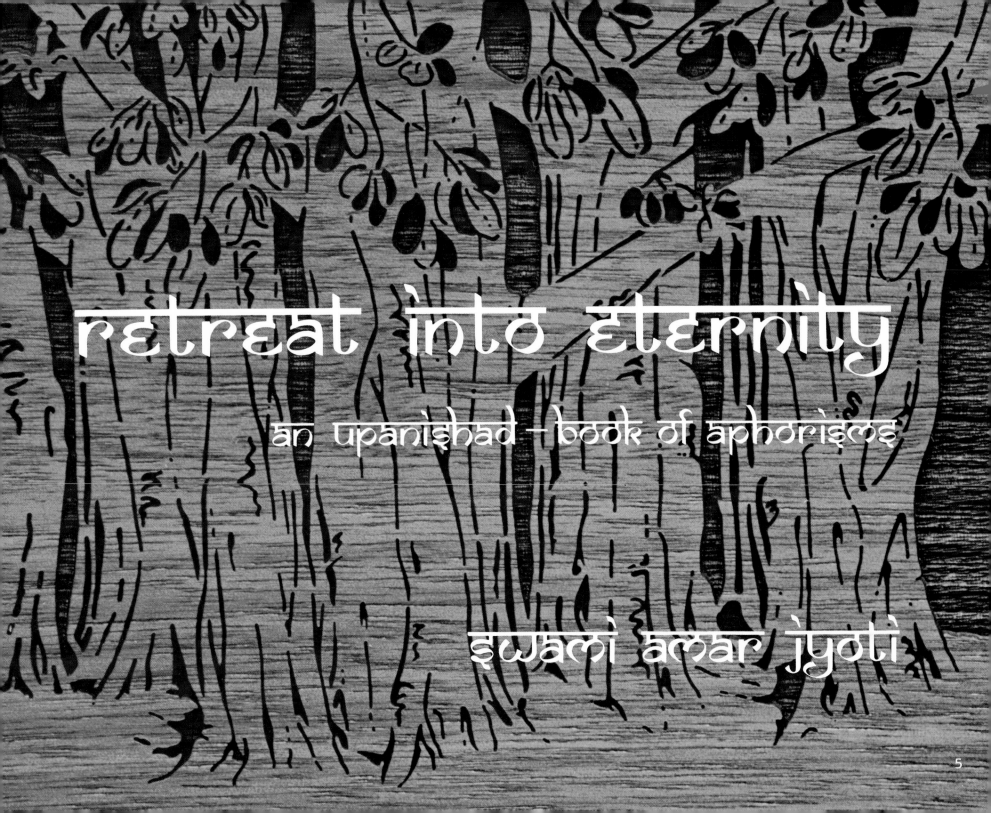

retreat into eternity

an upanishad—book of aphorisms

swami amar jyoti

By the same author:

Spirit of Himalaya — the story of a Truth seeker

DEDICATED TO THOSE WHO WANT TO KNOW

Library of Congress Catalog Card Number: 80-54236
Title: Retreat Into Eternity: An Upanishad — book of aphorisms
Published by:
        Truth Consciousness
        Gold Hill, Salina Star Route
        Boulder, Colorado 80302
        (303) 449-7660
Manufactured in the United States of America
ISBN 0-933572-03-4

AN UPANISHAD*

Spiritual knowledge is not a formal training; it is not like a class in which you sit and have lessons. Day to day, through each phase of his working, the Master imparts the training to the disciples. The Master is none else but your conscience. When you don't listen to your conscience then conscience comes out of you and, as it were, takes the embodiment of a Master and tells you the same thing.

Twenty-four hour dedication is needed for spiritual advancement. You have to be aware and ready for this. But unfortunately, the tendency is to keep it pending—for the next time, for the time when you will literally be sitting at the feet of the Master and will ask him about Enlightenment. Not only at that time, but also through all your experiences, through all your karmas, in whatever episodes, he is helping and guiding you toward Enlightenment, *provided you are open and receptive.*

*Sanskrit: lit. sitting near (the Master) to listen

Don't you see? Don't be afraid any more. Don't be a stranger any more. Don't hide any more. It's all God! Just *see* it and *be* it. And here, now it's suddenly safe enough, it's suddenly clear enough, there is suddenly love enough to dare to let go, to relax, to open to Him and let Him show us — what? Ourselves. Our True Self!

You don't have to remove the clouds to realize the space.
Where your consciousness lies you *see*.
Either you see the phenomena or you see the Reality.

All these journeys and discoveries have only been the
surface phenomena of changing formulas or forms on the
Substance. Realize this and be free.

As you change the conception, the pattern changes.
Remove all conceptions and you see the Reality, you come
face to face with pristine pure Consciousness.

Change yourself—the world will change.
Purify yourself—the world is sublime, divine.

Come back to your True Self. This is the sweet home, the real home. It is within you. It transcends senses, beyond pros and cons, beyond changing phenomena, evaluation. If you can do this you are wise. Such a one is called a sage. He is never perturbed, he is Enlightened, who under all conditions is in joy, whose compassion, love and mercy are inexhaustible.

Prophets and realized souls, saints and sages, come to fulfill us—not necessarily to fulfill all our wishes though.

These three are the most common factors among all the mystics and holy ones: their unflinching devotion and love for the Lord, for the people, and for the way of Truth.

It's your song, too.
You have just forgotten it.

Don't try to conquer;
realize unity.
Understand the difference.
There is nothing to win;
just *see* the unity.

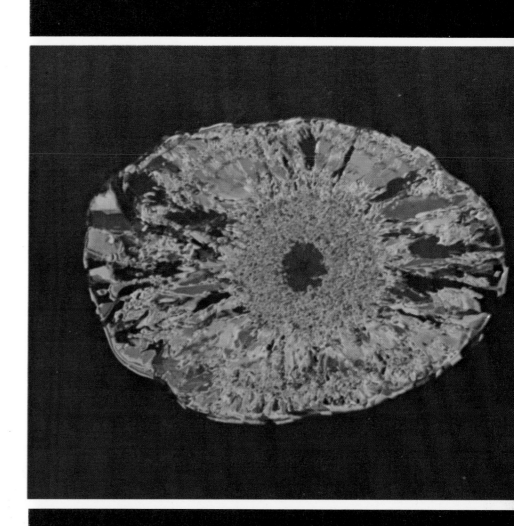

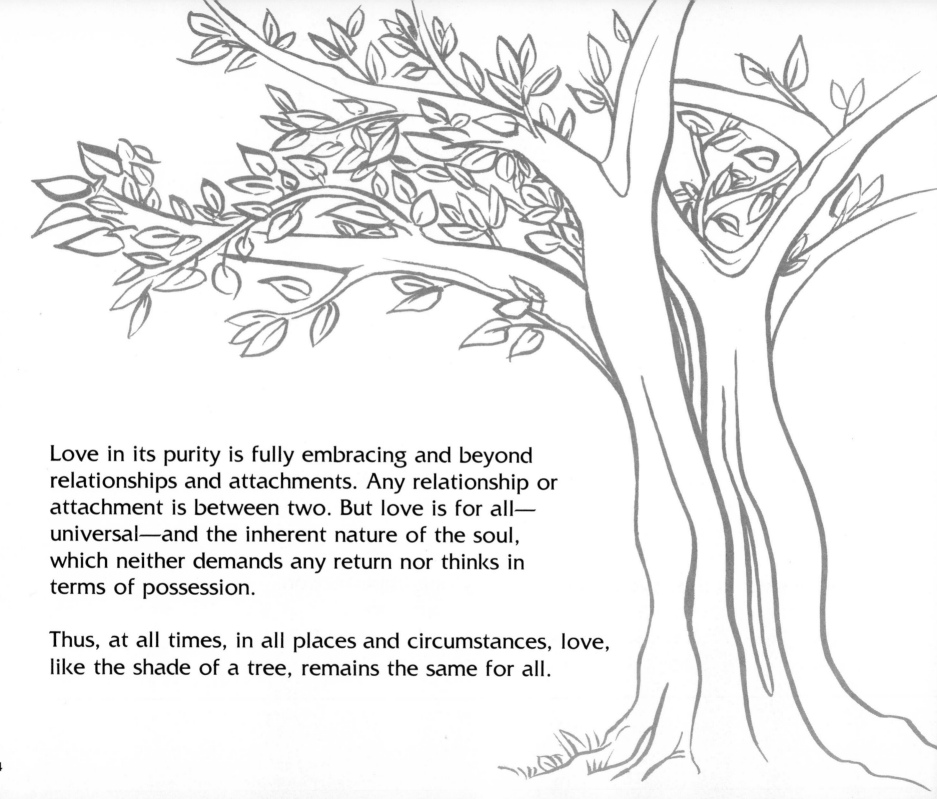

Love in its purity is fully embracing and beyond relationships and attachments. Any relationship or attachment is between two. But love is for all—universal—and the inherent nature of the soul, which neither demands any return nor thinks in terms of possession.

Thus, at all times, in all places and circumstances, love, like the shade of a tree, remains the same for all.

Why is it that just one drop of lemon can spoil millions of drops of milk in a pan? Why does one small piece of garbage make a place or thing unclean? Why does one evil make a whole human life miserable, a life which otherwise may be benevolent and happy? Why is it that when you hurt a person, one you might have loved continuously, the relationship may be disturbed or ended?

The answer is this: Even if there is only one imperfection and ninety-nine things okay, the whole Perfection is incomplete. And consciously or unconsciously, everyone is seeking Perfection.

All things you could understand very well: what the trees are communicating with each other, or the fish or the birds are telling each other. You don't have to know, but if you want to you can. There is not only an ecological but a cosmic interconnection of all things including ourselves. Barriers and divisions are a myth.

That all things are in you and you in all things—this is real Truth. When you will awaken to that subjectivity you'll know the Truth and see the beauty and joy in It.

Prayer is for your *own* opening
rather than to make God hear.
He already knows.

On the Divine Life plane
we need not teach ethics.
Ethics imperceptibly
follow the Divine.

Morality is the by-product
of spirituality.

Mind is divided into four compartments, in order to understand its workings: instinct, intellect, conscience and ego.

The *instinctive* mind is subject to the senses. When instinct arises, the mind says 'yes' or 'no' blindly, according to its likes and dislikes.

As man evolves, he becomes an *intellectual* or rational being. The intellect begins to control the instinct either by suppression or logic. If, however, the intellect follows the instinct, you are doomed to fall into a ditch if the latter is wrong, and blessed with safe passage if it is right. If the instinctive mind follows the intellect's determination to do or not do something, the instinctive mind is curbed or kept quiet. But there is no satisfaction in this, because the intellect has only the capacity to curb the instinctive mind or allow it free play.

Conscience, however, speaks from a deeper portion of the mind. It suggests whether you should or should not do something. It judges Truth from untruth, Real from unreal. The voice of conscience is the call of religion. It is the voice of conscience that guides the intellect and therefore the instinctive mind. The mind should not be ruled either by reckless instinct or limited logic, but by the conviction of what *should* or *should not be*.

The *ego*, the fourth portion of the mind, is simply the doer or director of the other three portions. Spiritual regeneration is easy when the ego listens to the conscience, which guides the intellect, which in turn purifies the instinct.

It needs heroic courage to decide that any habit is a bondage.

Habit is a dead branch on the tree of life. Life is creative and must remain so to give you joy.
When you let go of habits, illusions vanish. Ever new, spontaneous, conscious living is creative.

When you establish a habit, you make the mistake of repetition, which thickens the ego and forms your 'cherished' personality, which results in stagnation and death.

When you sit in meditation today, just remember one thing: that you are meditating today anew, because you have not *truly* meditated before. Don't practice habitually, but with the fresh attitude that you are meditating for the first time. This fresh approach lies beyond dogmas and traditions, beyond the usual ruts of your thinking. There is no repetition in nature. Don't lose sight of that ever-renewing Light, love for the real creative life.

The genesis of freedom is:
You are only free
when you let others be free.

Whatever you want, you should allow that freedom to others also. If this is true, then competition has no meaning. All you can do if you compete is supersede, and if you're doing that, you're violating the law of mutual freedom. You have freedom to progress in your own way, but in cooperation with others.

Letting others be free is also loving them. When you truly understand this, that only without a sense of possession can you love properly, you will have no fear and insecurity. Only then will your soul be free and joyful.

The spiritual path is a cleansing process.

Each one's mind being different, there cannot be a general path to follow. We should not be stereotyped into a uniform pattern of a path. That is an imposition from without, whereas spiritual unfoldment is from within.

When this unfoldment begins, it crosses each mind, and minds being different, they cannot unfold in the same way.

You, who are the creator of worries, worry.

When your hand is holding something, that thing is occupying your hand also. Similarly, when your mind clutches many things, rightly so many things are clutching your mind back. Don't forget it.

No God would ever wish that you work so much or in such a way that you forget Him.

Surrender to that One Who is blissful in Himself, Who is all in all, Who is the Light which ever shines—this is neither folly nor defeat. He is not asking too much. It is by virtue of His being everything that He is asking you to be nothing, because it is in becoming nothing that you become everything.

Whether you call it God or True Self or Spirit, ultimately, bowing to That, singing the glory and praise of the Lord, loving the Lord, is the highest religion. It's simply the culmination, the flowering of all the paths.

Joy is where the heart and mind settle.

Selfless action purifies the ego,
Devotion lessens the ego,
Meditation finishes the ego.

True peace comes from within
through the straightness and simplicity of Truth.

There is a divine breeze willing to guide the boat to port,
but the sailor in his agitation is setting the sails crooked.

Patience is waiting with a relaxed mind,
That things will happen as they should happen,
Not necessarily as we wish them to happen.

Spirituality is not what you want,
but what He wants.

There is no greater joy
than to be a fit vehicle of the Lord
                and His messengers.

It makes life sublime.

Those who live for the Lord are near Him.
Those who live for themselves are away from Him.

Once, I was on my way to Kedārnāth, one of the four main pilgrimages of Himalaya. Kedārnāth is about 12,000 feet above sea level and very cold. I was traveling on foot. On the way I saw many pilgrims, young and old, rich and poor, healthy and sick. Gorī Kund is a hot water spring at the last lap toward Kedārnāth, where pilgrims bathe and rejuvenate themselves before the final steep climb. There, among the pilgrims, was an old man who couldn't walk. He had jute cloth tied as padding on his feet, knees and hands to protect himself from the many stones. He crawled. I felt for this poor chap, and went up to him. He was an austere man with very kind eyes. I asked him, 'What is your name? Where are you from? . . .'

He answered, looking a little happy. He had come to the last lap toward Kedārnāth, which meant that the greater part of the journey was over. But still the climb would be very steep.

'Couldn't you go on horseback?'

'Well, no money. Could have been arranged, but thought it best this way.'

'What is your age?'

'About eighty.'

'Don't you feel cold, or afraid of dying?'

'Well, that's what I mean. If I die, it's okay . . . in Himalaya going toward Kedārnāth, what greater joy could there be!' Devotion was radiating in his eyes. I stood there a few moments and then resumed my journey.

After spending a week in Kedārnāth, I was starting on my way back when I met this old pilgrim in the street just as he neared the temple. It had taken him that long to reach there. I was happy to see him and he too. We knew each other, in a way.

You might say he was an insensible fool, but his eyes were shining with joy. I came up to him and asked how he was and whether he felt tired.

He said, 'No, I'm joyful. I'm nearing God, I'm going to reach and *see* Him!'

He had that full faith! Desires and worldly considerations were null and void for him. Whether he was a sage or not, God knows, but whatever he was, you cannot say he was crazy. Devotion and faith gave him the strength to go on. Call it grace. The grace of God can make the crippled cross mountains.

Just a little bit of a dazzling ray of God's grace in response
to your love for Him cancels all your ignorance, all
your deficiencies, setbacks, drawbacks, all your childish
games. Just in one moment.

Light is everywhere, even in the darkness of night. The dark space which we see between any two stars is fully radiant light. But why do we see it as darkness? Because our optical instrument called eye has limitations preventing us from seeing that Light. But if we could project our eye or another instrument, we would see that everything is light there. Just bright.

That formless space in between is more bright and dazzling than the forms of the stars we see; compared to it the stars are pale.

As a matter of fact, all the stars which are shining constitute only a little of the total light within space. If there was no light in the formless space, the light of the stars would have no possibility either.

Full with light He never sleeps—dazzling Light.
His power is a dynamo of energy
throughout the universe.

He radiates a clean kind of creation.
All that you see—the planets, stars and galaxies—
are projections out of Him.

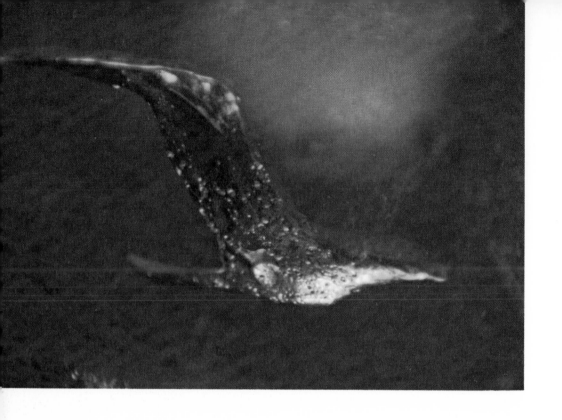

Realize your perfection
within
and you will see
everything is perfect.

Spiritual Consciousness
doesn't need trying,
it just needs realizing.

You have two wings with which to fly, but you have crippled
your wings in such a way that you have no wings now;
you remain heavy on earth, unable to fly up.
These two wings are timelessness and spacelessness.
Remove these two barriers—time and space—you'll fly,
instantly.

There is a silent cave, the
size and shape of the top of
your thumb, somewhere within
your brain, in the silence
of which the Light of
Consciousness shines.

Purity of the heart and
longing drill the path through
the spine to this
'Seat of the Soul'.*

*Pineal gland ('third eye')

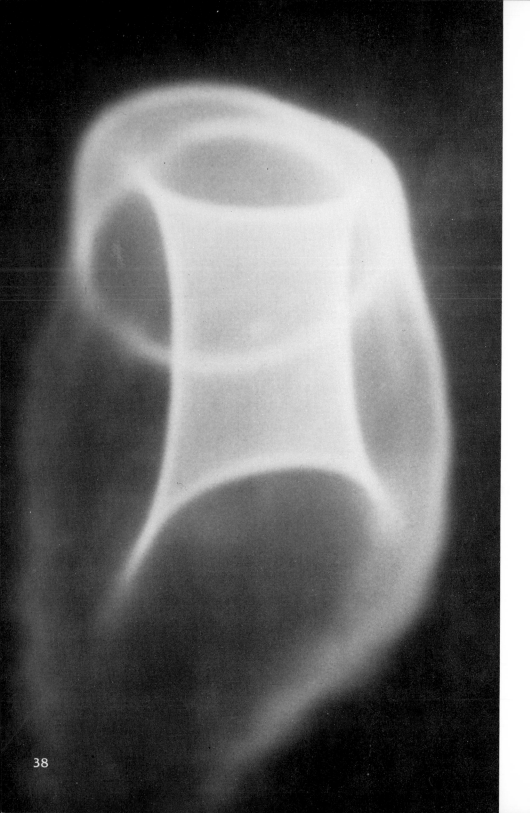

To the degree you've attained
    peace
you'll find it wherever you go.

To the degree you have faced
    the things in your mind
you'll be able to face
    things in the world.

To the degree you know yourself
you'll know the universe.

Letting-go is the best 'weapon' for gaining peace and happiness. Letting-go is not weakness or negligence, but simply a reflection that right and wrong are done by everyone. If with sincere efforts we cannot change someone, we may simply let-go and allow that one space to grow. This also maintains the law of mutual freedom and love.

When you retaliate, you are a man.
When you 'let go', you are divine.

Reason does not create faith.
Right reasoning arrives at faith eventually.
In other words,
faith is the true fruit of right reasoning,
not antagonistic to it.

Faith can create
a new planet altogether.

What is not within you is not outside either. What is within you is also outside of you. Even if you go to the moon or Jupiter or another galaxy—even another universe—there again your cry will be the same: to Know. Technology does not satisfy your cry.

First know your Self and there lies the secret of knowing everything.

Let the drop of 'i' merge in the ocean of 'I'.

If you want to cross the ocean of ignorance, it's so huge that to cross it seems impossible, even with the help of someone. But you don't have to cross it. Just sit where you are and go within yourself. Relax. Be still. There and then, Light will shine. You have crossed it.

Life is just an experience for consciousness with no more gain or loss in it.

God
is not an idea alone, please.
He is a real, living entity:
                    existence.

If He would not exist,
you and i would not exist.
The only folly is that
we have forgotten Him.
Even then,
look at the mercy of God:
                    we do exist!

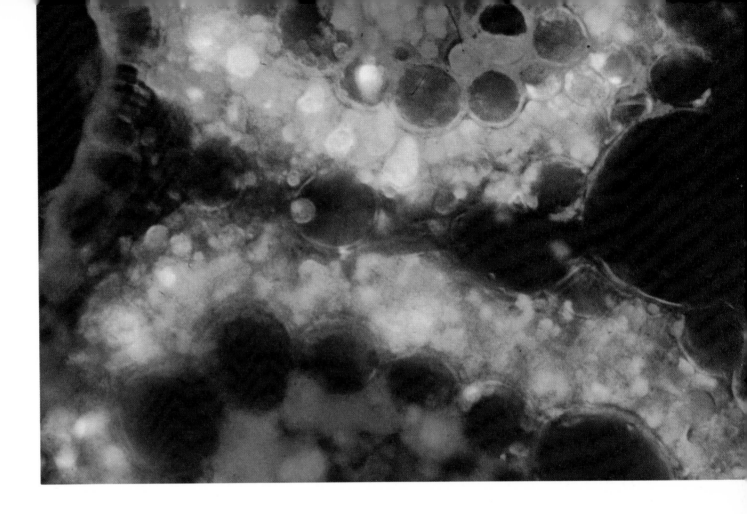

If God has ever created mysteries, there is only one:
that He kept the Reality enshrined in the cosmos
available to everyone, anytime, anywhere.

He has kept the macrocosm and microcosm within each other.

If you know your Self, you know the whole mystery.

The right path leads to the desired Goal.

It may not be comfortable, like traveling through deserts where the roads are lonely and dry. Once in a while a rest house comes up where there are some garbage cans, picnic tables, rest rooms and a place to park vehicles. And all around there is just the same road, same car, same tires, hour after hour.

But if you keep going, all of a sudden you will come to some green mountains where there are pine trees. You will begin to feel refreshed and happy and notice that the sweet wind is blowing, with birds in the breeze and animals grazing on green pastures.

God cannot change
the whole creation
to suit you.

You have to fit into His scheme.

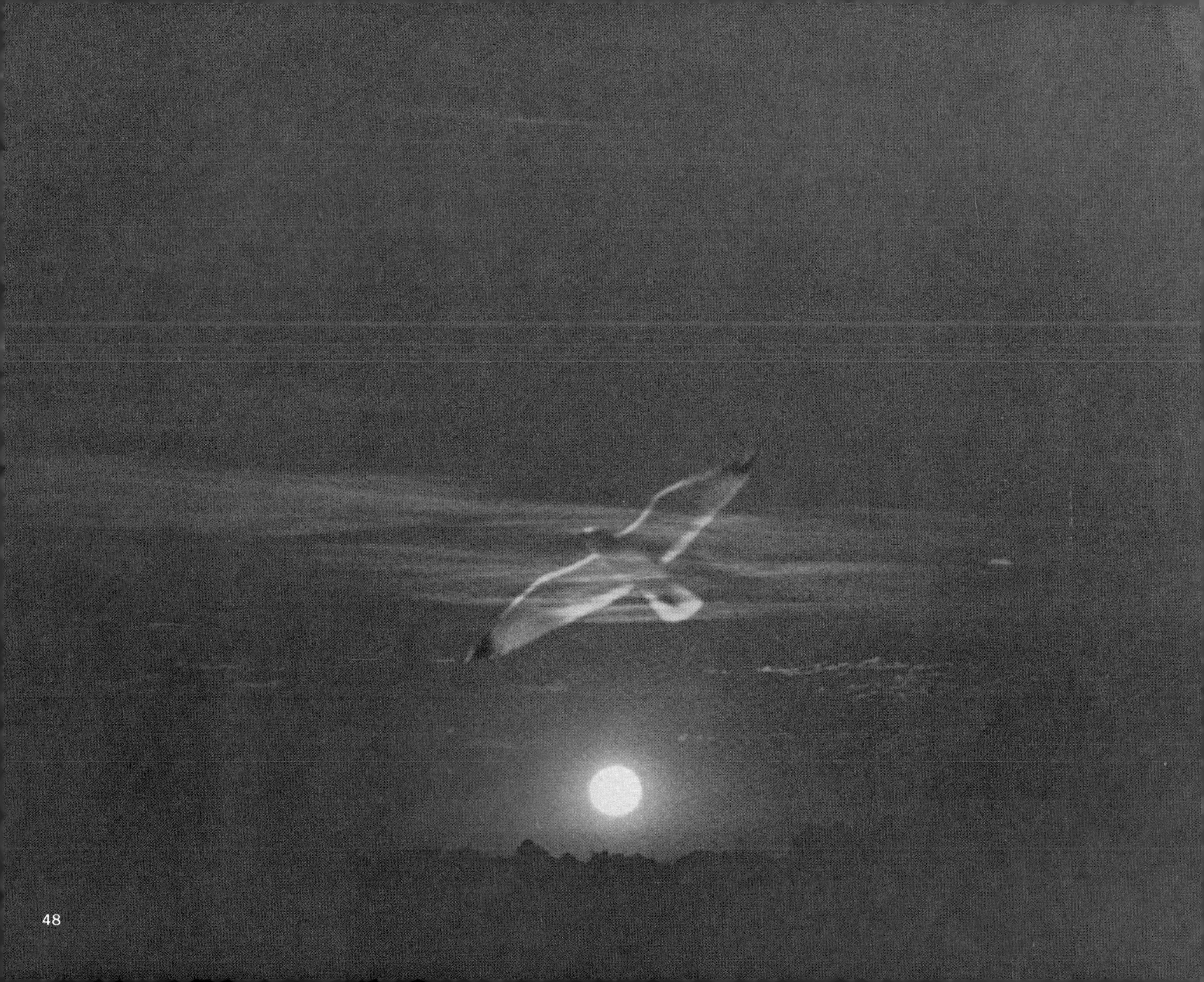

How is it that you do not flow with the fresh current of the river of life? Why is it that every time you sing or meditate, a beautiful river is not flowing through you?

By clutching to 'me', how could you fly freely? There is a continuity and wholesomeness in the cosmos, and you are a part of it. Without exception, all boredom and inadequacy are based on this separateness, the fictitious barrier of ego.

A 'fresh outlook' is where you are not assuming anything as it was before. Just see what it *is* and do not have preconceptions. You will find that you are seeing for the first time. Open your eyes: life is a perennial flow of joy, a perennial beauty.

We do not find perennial joy in life
because we are trying to seek it
without loving God—Who is the Light.

God's patience created time and space.

Be sure that God has given you all the possibilities
at any time, at any place, to know Him.

To be near Him you need two things: concentration of mind
and purity of heart.

The mission of every one on earth is to realize
his relationship with the Creator or the Source.
Why else did you come here?

In moments of silence and receptive moods, tears roll in gratitude for what God has done for us. At other times, it is hard to appreciate or see the point in it.

More stress is paid on an 'unconditional' attitude simply because the vision gets clearer thereby. By arguments and discussions, we hardly get a clear vision.

Love melts the heart and thus puts an end to all resistance. After all, what we need is a solution and satisfaction, right?

Reaching God or the Goal is not a mechanical process.
It is a very living, existential way.
It must be concrete, tangible, supremely alive.

The quality of the goal you choose
determines the quality of your life.

54

In the universe
where there's an abundance
of creation, how can we
even afford to have
insecurities? It's absurd.
Who has, after all,
created the sun and moon
and everything else
that sustains us?
And still we feel insecure!
There is only one reason
for this:
our selfishness.

People have practiced a routine for years and years, meaning very well perhaps, but they have forgotten the Goal. They are walking on a journey but have forgotten where they are going.

This forgetfulness makes you miss the secret of Oneness. It is all around you, it is within you, but you are searching and practicing for it. It is with you all the time, but you just do not allow it to be realized. You are resisting it, blocking it, obstructing it and philosophizing it.

Realize your Oneness with the cosmos which is already there within you.

Spirituality and science are the foundation
of all other aspects of life.

The best way to serve humanity is through spirituality and
science. This is a more proper solution than all the other
aspects together, whether religious, political, social,
economic or cultural, and the most lasting.

Whenever you wish to do anything, ask yourself if it has,
consciously, a spiritual and scientific base. If so, you will
never create problems.

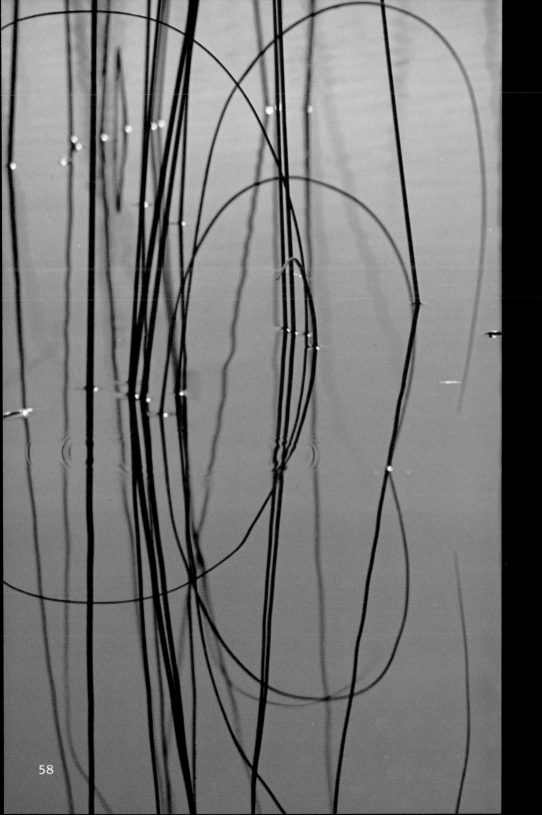

Often we lose sight
of the purpose
while entangled
in semantics.

Actually, common sense is most
uncommon—that's the problem.
Philosophy's abundant!

Absolute Truth is like the unbound sky
in which flight transcends paths.

You can only trust the things that are stable.
Truth is stable.

You have to leave the surface of the ocean
                                                    to reach the depths.
You have to leave the lowlands to reach the mountain peaks.

If you want to be peaceful,
the door can be opened by you alone.
Will it sincerely and go within.

Practices will make you confident;
Faith will give you strength;
Devotion will make you sublime.

Man came from God, created by Him and is always with Him. While being man he begins to believe 'I am a man', a separate conception. That conception of separateness is ego.

The biggest telescope is ego. Make it transparently clear, see through it, you'll see God.

You walk as one unit and talk and sleep. It is because of the inherent religious quality of your body constitution—certain laws which hold different component parts together as a sort of personality, as with a nation, a group, a building, an institution, a family, even molecules and atoms. This is called *dharma*, religion. The *way* you exist is religion.

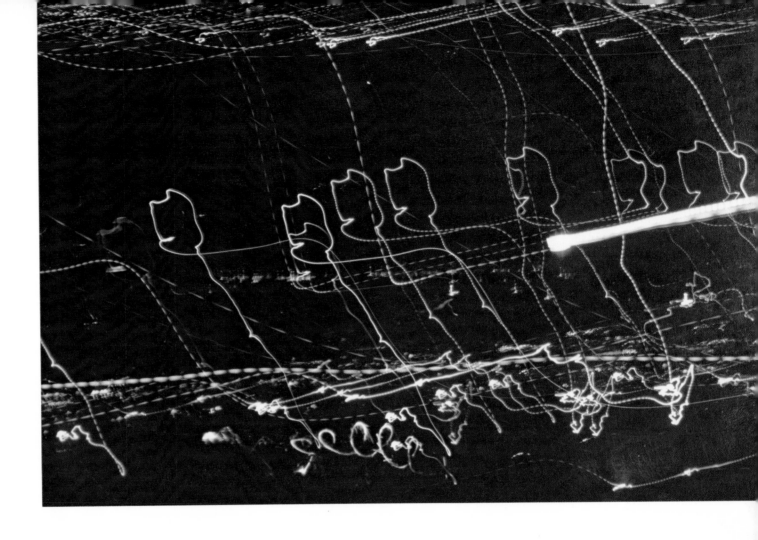

Life has endless progression. Whatever you desire creates its own domain of fulfillment, thus ever giving birth to newer creations which revolve in the same wheel of the world and around the same pivot which may be called the self.

Silencing is: demolishing the fantasy structures of the mind.

Beneath your skin there's no name. The leaf of a tree
under a microscope isn't called a leaf.
Likewise, when you go deeper into things, names change,
connotations change, the whole perception and
dimensions change until you come to that utter Silence
where there's no movement. That's release, immortality.

After all, what is outside and inside, except two sides of the same coin, the Self? The external self is ego, the internal one Spirit. But are these *really* two? Is not the outer self merely a reflection, a spark, a drop of the real Self which is an effulgent Sun, radiant Fire, a shoreless Ocean?

There are many waves on the surface of the ocean—thick and thin, big and small, forceful and weak. As you stand on the shore, quite a number of waves are near you, and as you penetrate your gaze beyond the near ones, you go further into other waves and still more waves. Often you are led away by the differentiation of the waves.

But if you just stand still for a second and divert your gaze from the phenomenal, changeful relativity, you will see only that sameness, that vastness—just water.

When the waves crash against the boulders on the seashore, they lose their form and get fragmented into many pieces. Water remains water. It is neither hurt nor anxious. The simple, direct method to realize this is: 'God, not me, Thee, for Thou art the Substance. I am Thy shadow and creation. Thou art the Reality, my True Self.'

You may deny God only in conception, not in reality. God doesn't vanish by your denial. Water won't vanish if you deny it in the wave. The Spirit or Light within you is not extinguished even if you cover it up.

There is only one way to Truth and ninety-nine to untruth. Truth lies in oneness.

With due respect to your 'free will', if you are experimenting with Truth, you are trying to retain the ego, to prolong the habit of ignorance. *You do know Truth.* Those who are humble enough will admit that they are denying Truth, knowingly or unknowingly. Have you sincerely accepted Truth in your heart and not merely in notebooks and diaries? Who can remedy your confusion if you deny Truth with your own free will?

Be truthful to the core of your being and you will find freedom of the soul in no time.

Your own creative ideas are the best confirmation of the Truth,
for they give you the incentive to seek and find It yourself.

When your consciousness
identifies with the Absolute
you find all your answers.
It is in the vast open space,
in that wilderness,
the virgin land that you find
the source of creation.
In Infinity all these
finitudes are made.
When you rest in this purity
and virginity of your Spirit
you know the secret.

Mere determination cannot do everything,
if it is exclusive of humility.

To be humble is to be courageous.
When you have the humility to see your own weaknesses,
that is when courage comes in.

Humility is not wishing, even if you deserve;
Arrogance is wishing, even if you do not deserve;
When you deserve more, you expect the least.

Be courageous to face God,
and you will be cleansed
and brightened in His radiance.

Distance and delay have been
created by you and your
unjustified demands.
The Lord is never away from you.

When you see yourself you do not see God;
When you see God you don't see yourself.

Only renouncing 'free will' is not the answer.
It has to be merged in His will.

God is such a mold that when you pour yourself into Him
He sends you out in His own image.

In love of God there is love for all;
In devotion to God there is compassion for all;
In surrender to God there is oneness with all.

You begin to think only when you have lost the capacity to *see*.

Perfect love will open your eye to wisdom
in such a way that you will *see* rather than think.

It is your 'free will' to hide your eyes with the palm of your hand and negate the sun or not.

You could keep God away millions of years
if you so choose.

There is a staircase of a hundred steps leading to a rooftop on which there is a heavenly garden. You may climb ninety-nine steps, but if you do not take the hundredth one, you miss the whole garden—the Perfection. Before you say, 'I love You, God', reflect twice—reflect ten times. Ask yourself, 'Is my love unconditional, perfect?' If it is, you will bask in the sublime sunshine of His Presence.

If you strike a match against a matchbox, light shines.
Where does it come from? Why doesn't water flow?
Because Light is everywhere, water is not.
Ultimately, the secret is Light, Consciousness, the
Substance of water and other elements too.

Pinch anywhere in the universe, Light will shine. Just open
the veil a little bit. The whole universe is such a ripe fruit
that wherever you pinch juice comes out. Light is
everywhere, within you, without you. Just concentrate.

Be what you *really* are.

Instead of trying to draw a line between finite and infinite
Consciousness, which can never happen, you have to merge
the finite into the Infinite, because it's already a part of It.

In each drop there is water
In each ray there is light
In each spark there's fire
In the same way, each creature
    has the Creator in him.

How does the Creator look after billions of holograms? He just creates them and leaves them in space and they, somehow, find out their own place. All the galaxies, the planets and stars are in their own positions because of gravitational pull; by some kind of calculations they find their own place and fit in.

You are where you are because of your doings. You have found your own position, dangling somewhere and being pulled from five different directions—two degrees north and four degrees south, in longitude and latitude, geographically! It's your choice; it's your creation.

But in spite of this, you could still be equipoised where you are, just by relaxing and being still.

When you wait upon God, you don't know that you're becoming God.

Once you were Enlightened, now you are un-enlightened. How did you lose the Light? If you could discover the secret to this mystery, it would be easy to achieve It. The way you lost It will be the way to regain It.

A ghost went into a bottle. Now the problem is, how to bring it out without breaking the bottle? It has to be taken out the way it went in. By streak of imagination you sent the ghost into the bottle; just by imagination bring it out. Will it.

Didn't you will something other than Enlightenment? That is why you lost It. When you desired otherwise, it happened, because an Enlightened soul is omnipotent. Then from one desire you tumbled down to the second, the third, eventually the millionth and you *forgot* where you began the journey. And now you say you don't know. Just aspire sincerely to be Enlightened, you will regain It.

In the same way, if you took the elevator down from the fourth floor, you go back by the same elevator. You cannot sit on the first floor weeping, saying 'How am I to go up?' You have to take the same elevator, the elevator of will, the elevator of aspiration.

Unless you had lost Enlightenment, how could you play? So you shut out the Light. In darkness you have pleasures; in Light you have Joy. Enlightenment is Light—It knows no darkness. Perfection knows no imperfections.

Truth knows no compromise. If you don't compromise, it is very easy.

Do not give excuses that society makes it too difficult for you to be truthful. Truth has its own energizing capacity: the more you live it, the more it gives you strength.

It is your self-complacency and disbelief which make you think that you cannot be truthful in a society which is otherwise. This shows the common weakness of following what others do, even if it may be against principle.

Certain trials and challenges beset you. But the more you accept the tests, the more powerful you become. Truth does bestow strength.

There is no solution
within the relative thinking
of B and C.

You are lost until you bring in
the Absolute point: A
joined with 'you' and 'me'.

You may play your part
in the cosmic machinery
but while maintaining your
consciousness with your Creator.
Then only will you understand
the whole secret of creation.

Be sure you will never be satisfied
until you realize the *true* nature
of your existence.

Life is Yoga.
All parts of the being—physical,
psychological and spiritual—
are necessary ingredients
of life on earth.
The grounds, the temple building
and the deity inside
are all sacred.
So don't neglect any department
of your house.
Be conscious every moment,
in each place.
This is Yoga.

Be open and receptive to find refuge in God. He will wash you quickly like a mother does with a naughty child. Even though the mother may have warned the child, 'Don't go out, don't get dirty, don't do this, don't do that, you'll spoil your clothes, you'll soil the house, today guests are coming and I've arranged everything so don't spoil it,' still, the child might pull the tablecloth and the dishes fall down. Or he may go into the bathroom and start putting the soap into the bathtub, towels fall down and the water goes on running and the plastic tub curtain hangs lop-sided, and so on. The mother then rebukes and spanks the child and he begins to cry, 'Mama, Mama, you don't love me!' The Mama replies, 'Do you know what you have done, kiddy?!' Even then, the loving mother takes the child up and washes, cleans and sets all things right.

If we are childlike, simple—that's a must, M U S T—and approach God the Father or God the Mother and pray honestly and sincerely, everything will be cleansed.

Love is felt by another being, whether it is a baby or an animal or a bird or a plant. All respond to love. But attachment squeezes. We normally think this attachment form of love is what others need. No.

If you had a scientific instrument with which to analyze vibrations of attachment you would see that they shrink the consciousness of both parties.

Attachment is bondage and a decaying process. Love is enlivening, inspirational and liberating.

The more you expand, the more you live. When you're unlimited, you're immortal.

When you touch a point where
you feel love tangibly for God, the Creator,
your personal identity
begins to merge into the cosmic,
individual soul touches the Universal Soul.

You're at one with all, at peace.
You become conscious.

In the night when you lie down with your head on the pillow, with humility and sincerity ask Him His will. He'll speak to you, in that ear which is pressed against the pillow, which is not likely to hear outside.

He'll let you know what His will is.

Let God do His will. He'll guide you perfectly if you love Him genuinely.

Freedom of the soul has no laws.
It is a law unto itself.

Freedom is not over others;
it is within yourself.

Freedom has no meaning
   if it is not for all.

The truly religious man is he
whose soul is free for God.

God has made us free. Be sure.

Ego is the noose in which you hang
as long as you keep forgetting
the Light that is within you.

There is no greater hell than doubts.
Faith is the temple of virtues.

In death is always a new life.

If you want to get rid of fear and be courageous, take each thing in itself. Any person, situation, problem, property, relationship—try to look at each in itself and not in comparison with something else.

We are habituated generally to knowing a thing by comparison and relationship to something else. Therefore we go on changing our opinions according to the things we compare with, and then those in turn change, changing our opinions again.

The only solution is to look at each person, relationship and thing individually. You can know any thing only in itself. The time you will be aware of this, fear will leave you.

Receive the Truth, keep you mind on It, and go into silence.
Be like an oyster, which takes the drop of rain water,
closes its shell, and dives to the bottom of the ocean.
There the drop becomes a pearl.*
Penetrate through your subconscious mind
to the depth of your being, and your Spirit will shine.

*This is according to Indian legend.

That's the way it should be
—your feet on earth,
your consciousness
with your Lord.

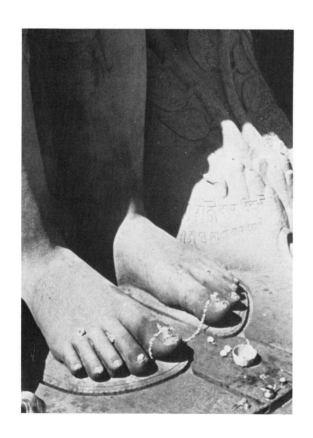

Suppose you are six feet tall and you are going to be ten.
Do you lose your six feet?

Man is included in the superhuman;
the whole creation is included in the Supreme Creator.

But that *fear* of losing the limitations—that is the tragedy.

There is not a single misery
in the world which is real.
There is not a single pain
on the whole earth which is
created by the Creator.
Any pain in your life is due
to separateness, or misconception
of separateness from the Creator.
There is no real pain and misery
involved, if you take it from
the Creator's viewpoint,
the cosmic view.

Actually, 'troubles' have
a two-fold purpose
in the Divine play.
They are the fruits
of past misdeeds,
and at the same time,
they purify the dross
and open inner potentialities
of strength and wisdom.

The time when you are trying to avoid, to escape, to suppress, to make something look different than it actually is, or to happen differently than it naturally does, you remain unconscious and ignorant of the Reality.

The world is simply a symbolic reflection of your own mind —not one percent less, not one percent more.

The ultimate goal of life is to know life, not just to enjoy it.

The Ultimate Reality—who will investigate It? Something apart from It? Something over and above the Reality must investigate the Reality and prove It? Is this not a fallacy? If you were apart from the Substance you could explore It. But if you are a part of that Substance, how are you going to explore It? In other words, Reality or Realization is beyond the scope of proof or investigation. It's a matter of *being*.

You are the 'doer' is the problem. As long as you are believing you are the doer, you are creating a wall between yourself and God—a myth, thus creating problems superfluously.

Light radiates joy
Consciousness bestows peace
Wisdom fulfills.

The Ultimate is not to be
practiced—It unfolds.

You have to be bold in mind
to not be threatened by the frankness of Truth.
There is no darkness if you face the sun.

The horizon of your consciousness and truthfulness
determines the extent of your *being*. The extent to which
you exist even now is due to Truth, not untruth. Your life is
integrated in direct proportion to the degree that you are
truthful. When your consciousness is boundless and totally
open, you are fully liberated and enlightened.

If you're not feeling free, it's only because you're not truthful.

We deliberately or unconsciously or semi-consciously blind ourselves and say, 'We don't know what is Truth'. This is self-deception. It is easy to know the Truth, if we are bold, sincere and honest. Each mind knows subconsciously, if not on the surface, what is Truth.

Truth is simple, Truth is One, Truth is transparent, Truth is as clear as daylight, Truth is God, Truth is Love, Truth is Light and so on. If Truth is so simple, how can it be so difficult to understand?

We do not understand the Truth or catch the Truth or see the Truth, not because it is difficult but because of other reasons. What other reasons? Because if we *really* recognize and accept the Truth and face it, we are bound to lose the false sense of possessiveness, pride of position, the sticky muddiness of greed, anger and attachments, and subsequently superfluous ego. Knowing this in the subconscious mind, out of fear we pose to not know the Truth.

You twinkle too much
and forget that it is
the Ultimate God
Who gives Light.

In humility unity resides.

True knowledge lies in being one
with that which you want to know.

Divine vision radiates in egolessness. Unless the seed dies, the tree is not born. Ego has to dissolve in order for the Divine to manifest.

The Divine is the best insurance, but His premium is high: ego.

Life is divine and it is worth living
                                 as a prayer to the Lord.
Beauty is a poem sung by the Lord
                                 and it is in your eyes.
Works are devotion in manifestation
                                 and those are worth accomplishing.

In a village, there was a pond. It was a silent pond. I used to contemplate the sun and moon in that pond.

One day a lady came with a pitcher—as is the custom to fetch water for cooking and drinking. When she waded in knee-deep to collect clean water farther from the bank, the surface of the water became wavy with ripples, all those circles of water. The sun became wavy too. Then at times I couldn't see the sun because—as I later understood—my attention went to the waviness of the water. And as soon as I again concentrated on the sun it was already there. The lady came out with the pitcher and went away.

I waited patiently, allowing the time to lapse. The water got still, silent. The sun was shining again. That's meditation.

Light shines in the peaceful mind.

You can only be one-pointed
on one point.

Just face it—whatever it is—
and see the Truth.
You will see,
if you are so bold to look at it,
that the ghost will vanish.
You won't have to kill the ghost,
you won't have to defeat it.
There is no ghost!

God is within the chamber
of your own heart.
There is a golden gate
to which the Master
shows you the way.
But you yourself
must open the gate
and meet your Lord.

How many are those who are lovers of God
for whom God means everything
for whom God is life?

There is pure satisfaction in this praise-prayerful life, for what greater task in life is there than to glorify the Lord? It is the fulfillment of all endeavors and ambitions and cravings. Surely it purifies all the layers of your being and makes you dance in ecstasy.

Love is indefinable. I could explain it to you only by loving you.

The silence within us is the source of all that we are.

Each one of us seeks something which we could term, 'That's it!' We are seeking something about which we could say, 'This is full and perfect', or to which silence would be the only answer.

Each moment is a center
each particle is a center
center of the Truth and Consciousness
therefore blissful always, everywhere.

Remember Light and It shall enlighten you.
Concentrate on Bliss and It shall make you blissful.
Take care of Truth and It shall take care of you.

Tap the right spring source; water will flow.

That spring of Light is within you—
of Truth, beauty, joy and consciousness.

Meditate upon It and realize.

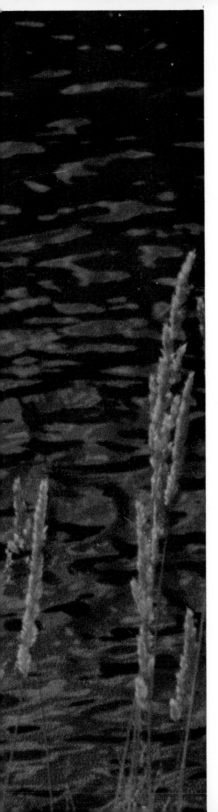

'I am a wave—one day I shall become water.'
This is the first fallacy.
Realize the essential unity.

Everything is within you.
All this is within you.
You willed and it became manifest.
It is Pure Consciousness playing in myriad forms.

Retreat into eternity and awake in ecstasy.

ACKNOWLEDGEMENTS:

BOOK DESIGN by the author
    Layout assistance: Ronnye Russell
                    Jerald Reames
    Production assistance: Ronnye Russell
                          S. Stuhlmiller

PHOTO CREDITS
Barstow, Nancy 30, 31, 93, 116, 117, 120
Bruwer, Andre-Skiagraphics 64, 118
Elkin, Lynne 45
High altitude Observatory of the National Center for
   Atmospheric Research (NCAR), Boulder, Colorado 13, 76
Jyoti Ashram (India) 98
Killeen, Alan 18, 41, 50, 54, 55, 59, 63, 70, 74, 88
   and front cover
Kominsky, Carl 8, 58
NASA 37, 51
Official U.S. Navy Photograph: 34, 35 and back cover (art by
   Jerald Reames)
Reames, Jerald 38, 47, 78, 115
Reese, Ron and Bonnie 33, 92
Reeves, Randy 12
Rishi Ashram (Himalaya) 22
Russell, Ronnye 16, 69
Stuhlmiller, S. 9, 36, 44, 62, 66-67, 81, 84, 87, 96, 110, 113,
   121, 124, 126
Zion—National Park Service 94
Courtesy: T.C. Journal 20, 24, 28, 72, 100, 101, 105, 107, 109,

Composition by the author:
   48, photos by S. Stuhlmiller,
      Pat Gilbo
   85, photos by Nancy Barstow,
      S. Stuhlmiller

ART CREDITS
Title pages 4-5 (designed by the author)
   Drawing by Jerald Reames; woodcutting by Lasercraft.
Reames, Jerald: 35 and back cover (Official U.S.
   Navy Photograph)

ABOUT THE AUTHOR

In the true spirit of the Upanishads, the aphorisms in this book were originally the personal communication of the Master to the disciples, whether spoken in various Satsangs or written in His countless letters. Such truths when communicated in this way carry with them a power and immediacy that ring through the printed page.

Swami Amar Jyoti's way with each person is individual. His vision is so boundless and yet unified that he can chart each seeker's varied path to the Goal. Whether we call it God, Consciousness, Light or Truth is immaterial to the One Who manifests and resides in it, and the utter love and serenity of his being through any circumstances communicates to us beyond labels and intellectual differences. As Swamiji has said, *'We search for who we are in One Who Is.'*

In Swamiji's presence, things we thought to be separate questions or problems are exposed in the light of the highest Truth. We are challenged to drop our preconceptions and bask in the clear atmosphere of illumination, having nothing to lose but our ignorance. With playful humor and loving wisdom, he coaxes us to the limits of our understanding and then opens the skylight of consciousness onto the vast 'knowable' cosmos of the inner Self, to give each reader at least a glimpse into Eternity.

Swamiji is the Founder-President of two Ashrams in India and four in the United States including two communities for lay disciples. Born in 1928 in India, he first came to the United States in 1961 and from 1973 onward his work has kept him mainly in the U.S.

the publishers

INDEX

You do not become an open book before God just to ask for a few more chapters in it!